how to read
your cat's mind

Purring Matters

how to read
your cat's mind

Celia Haddon

Little Books by Big Names™

For Jasper

First published in the United Kingdom in 2003 by Little Books Ltd,
48 Catherine Place, London SW1E 6HL

10 9 8 7 6 5 4 3 2

Text copyright © 2003 by Celia Haddon
Design and layout copyright © 2003 by Little Books Ltd

A CIP catalogue record for this book is available from the British Library.

ISBN: 1 904435 06 8

*Many thanks to: Jamie Ambrose for editorial management, Eluned Jones
for editorial assistance, Ghost for original jacket styling and illustration,
Mousemat Design for jacket and text design, Margaret Campbell of Scan-Hi
Digital and Craig Campbell of QSP Print for printing consultancy, Angie
Hipkin for indexing, and to William, Mog & Jasper, and the other good cats
who made this book possible. Printed and bound in Scotland by Scotprint.*

contents

introduction   7

1   how to read your cat's instincts   11

2   how to understand what your cat is saying   33

3   how to help your cat learn   55

4   how to look after your pedigree cat   75

5   how to protect your cat's territorial rights   93

6   how to solve your cat problems   115

7   how to pamper your elderly cat   139

    a word about disabled cats   154

    useful numbers & acknowledgements   156

    index   158

*For I am possessed of a cat, surpassing
in beauty, from whom I take occasion
to bless Almighty God.*
CHRISTOPHER SMART
(1722–1771)

introduction

Love is... hearing your cat purring. Like the half-shut eyes and the rough, painful touch of a cat's tongue, purring means all is well in our world: the world of the cat-human bond. And, as this mysterious vibration reaches our ears, we would purr back – if only we could.

What a gulf separates us – the upright apes who travel in space – from the small, desert carnivores who cannot even use words.

Yet love spans this great divide, linking two vastly different species in a mutually affectionate relationship. We spend our lives together, most of the time with contentment. Indeed, the cat-human relationship often works better than a marriage.

Does your cat properly understand you? It probably does – well enough, at least, for its own purposes. It can lead you to the fridge, remind you of mealtimes and share your bed in cold nights.

Do you understand your cat? Probably not as well as it understands you – which is why this book has been developed: to help you read your cat's mind. It will explain the cat's basic instincts, the way it talks and what it means; how, what and when it learns. It will outline what a cat needs in order to have a happy home, and it will explain some of the most common misunderstandings that occur in the cat-human relationship so that you can make your cat happy.

It will also outline some of the special needs of pedigree cats, and of cats kept indoors. And finally, it will help you pamper and better understand your elderly cat.

Whatever its age, it is the happiness of your cat that really matters.

*The cat is domestic only as far
as it suits its own ends.*
SAKI
(1870–1916)

1

how to read
your cat's instincts

The cat that sleeps on your bed and lies upside down under your central-heating radiators is actually a relative newcomer to human family life. Unlike the dogs, horses, cattle and sheep which have been domesticated for thousands of years, cats moved in only recently.

It was 6,000 years ago at the most – not very long in evolutionary terms. And we didn't domesticate them. They 'domesticated' themselves, walking into our lives only when there were enough mice and rats in human settlements to make it worthwhile for them to do so.

Indeed, you could even argue that it was *they* who domesticated *us*. They get shelter and cat food, and in return they haven't had to change many of their habits.

We are the ones who have changed. The relationship was originally a functional one – the cat kept human premises free of rodents, and in return, received shelter and, occasionally, a little food.

Dogs were man's best friend. Cats were merely useful rodent operatives.

Early writers complained that cats were more attached to places than people, that they showed no signs of gratitude or love for humans. They were necessary workers rather than members of the family.

But lately, we have fallen in love with cats. It has taken a few thousand years for them to persuade us, but now they don't even have to pay for their board and lodging by doing the mousing.

Clever cats: we give and they take. How did they pull off this amazing trick?

YOUR CAT'S ANCESTRY

If you want to understand the sheer cunning of the cat, you have to know a little about its ancestry. Your cat, even if it has a posh pedigree, is still wild at heart.

The domestic cat evolved from the African wild cat about 4,000 to 6,000 years ago. The original cat ancestor still flourishes. It is more or less the size of a domestic cat, with a coat varying from grey to tan. It is not a spectacular animal (like a lion), and it's difficult to track, so we don't know much about it.

We do know that the female cats live in with their kittens until these are old enough to leave the family group. But while lions hunt in family parties in order to pull down game as big or bigger than themselves, the African wild cat kills mainly rodents, some birds and other small animals. There's no reason for group hunting, as a single mouse isn't big enough to feed a group.

The wild cat is a cat that hunts by itself. And this affects cat behaviour. A wolf needs its pack in order to kill for food, so it learns many social behaviours needed for group living. Home is where the pack is. Not so for the African wild cat.

The males roam widely, more or less on their own, while the females live with their kittens. But, as far as we know, adult African wild cats have never lived together in large communities.

Establishing core territory

The wild cat needs a territory, not a pack. Home is an area within a wild cat's territory where it is safe – its kittening dens and its places to sleep during the day. This is the core territory.

Further out are its hunting grounds, its home range, where it can hunt without too much competition from others. If prey is scarce, this territory will be big, up to four kilometres (or approximately two-and-a-half miles). If there are lots of rodents around, it will be a small area.

At the edge of its territory will be the boundaries, points where other cats may be found – either competing females or males roaming in search of sex. There is little to see on these boundaries, but the African wild cat, like all cats, will leave scent marks of various kinds. As territory will always be more important for its survival than social bonds, it needs to mark boundaries.

How the wild cat came in from the cold

Many cat species are solitary hunters, but the African wild cat is different even from the other small wild cats. It can be tamed. Other cats, like the very similar European wild cat, stay aloof when they grow up, even if they are reared by humans. However, an African wild cat reared by humans seems to accept them as family.

Nonetheless, from the beginning, when the first African wild cats began to live near or in human settlements, their relationship to humans was very different from that of the other domesticated animals.

Cattle are herded or penned up, then eaten by men. Dogs were used by early man as guard dogs and as hunting assistants – yet the game they pulled down was primarily to feed men and they just got the bits left over. The pack instinct had betrayed them into obeying human instructions.

Cats never did. The less frightened ones moved into human settlements of their own accord, and were welcomed for their ability to get rid of the mice and rats that overran grain stores. Yet humans couldn't exploit the cat's hunting activities for the larder. Humans wanted bigger game than mice!

So cats were left to hunt on their own (just as they did in the wild). They were not trained, controlled, tied up, or put in cages or fields. They lived side by side with human beings, each species conferring a benefit on the other. It was a remarkably equal relationship. It still is.

Domestic cats who live in the wild

Of course, today's cats are no longer African wild cats. Despite their independent personality, domestication has changed them, both physically and mentally. Their coat comes in different colours, and they are no longer entirely solitary by nature; feral and stray cats prove that. If there is enough food, such as a nearby rubbish dump or a friendly feeder, they will live together, not in a pack, but in family groups within large colonies.

Perhaps this group living, which means that cats live happily in human families, is a change brought about by domestication. Or perhaps the African wild cat had this potential, but its lifestyle – catching small rodents in desert areas – made any group living impossible. Another possibility is that domestication effectively encouraged juvenile behaviour – and it is natural for juvenile cats to live with their mother in a little family.

Eating habits may also have changed the domestic cat. The true African wild cat rarely scavenges carrion and does not feed on rubbish dumps, yet domestic cats are found on rubbish dumps throughout the African wild cat's territory. They have developed a digestive system able to cope with dumped food.

Today's domestic cats have the ability to live in social arrangements which would not suit a wild cat. Many live happily in multi-cat households, sharing beds and grooming each other. Even so, some individuals are happier living as a single pet.

How your cat is hard-wired

Your own petted and pampered feline shares the same instincts as its wild ancestor – instincts which are hard-wired into its brain. There are three of these:

- the instinct to have sex and reproduce,
- the instinct to hunt,
- the instinct to avoid danger.

Unless you understand that these three instincts shape your cat's lifestyle, you will never properly understand your furry loved one. These instincts are common to all cats everywhere: pampered pets, posh pedigrees, street strays, lonely ferals. A cat is always a cat.

The mating instinct

The powerful instinct to mate in order to reproduce is now under human control via the veterinary practices of neutering and spaying. These drastic measures of stopping the instinct at source are the only way of taming the cat's roving libido. Cats which are not neutered are escape artists when in search of sex – as the small ads for 'pedigree-cross kittens' reveal.

Most domestic pets are not allowed to breed, but the ready supply of kittens at cat rescue shelters, often the offspring of stray or feral cats, suggests that nothing we humans do is seriously going to reduce the worldwide domestic cat population. We snip, but kittens still rule.

Yet neutering and spaying are essential for those who want a relaxed and close relationship with a pet. In a world where thousands of cats end up in rescue shelters, it is selfish to insist on yet another litter of kittens just for human amusement.

Besides, un-neutered tom-cats are noisy

and smelly, and roam around looking for copulation, getting into fights as a result. Female cats are so extraordinarily fertile that a single female can produce 200 kittens in her lifetime. If all the kittens survived, there would be as many as 65,536 extra cats in the world five years later.

Neutering allows our cats to enjoy the deep peace of the warm house instead of the hurly-burly and excitement of life and love on the rooftops.

True sexual behaviour is not able to survive the neutering process, but some of the reproductive behaviour – mothering kittens, for instance – remains. Cats will employ mother-kitten behaviour in the cat-human relationship, treating us either as kittens or mother cats.

Understanding the hunting instinct

Your cat – and every cat – has the mind of a murderer. It is designed as a killing machine. Cats *have* to eat meat. Their digestive systems simply can't get enough nourishment out of a vegetarian diet.

So a cat has to kill to live in the wild, and nature has programmed it to live to kill. We feed our cats lavishly so that they have no survival need to hunt for food. Yet nature hasn't caught up with tinned cat food, and our dearest puss is still a killer at heart. There's no need to starve cats to make them better hunters. Faced with a mouse, the best-fed cat in the world will catch and kill it.

Hunting is innately rewarding for cats. The actions resulting from the hard-wired instinct fire up the happiness section of the feline brain. Your cat doesn't have to catch any prey to enjoy it. Even if it is an indoor cat that has never seen a mouse, it still enjoys play-hunting.

The hunting programme, installed by nature into the cat's brain, is a set sequence of moves. These are made in serial order, one action succeeding another. The sequence is eye, stalk, pounce and grab, bite, tear and eat (see page 30). All of these actions are immensely fulfilling for the cat performing them. For a cat, happiness is doing what it has to do.

Understanding the killing instinct

The series is compulsive. Each action follows another. Sometimes, a move can't be performed until all the previous moves have preceded it.

Watch your cat making a pounce that fails to locate the prey. It rarely pounces again immediately. It is much more likely to go back to move one (eyeing its prey), do a shortened version of move two (the stalk), and then pounce.

The need for the predatory sequence to stay in order also occurs when a well-fed domestic cat grabs the prey, but fails to kill-bite it, perhaps because it isn't hungry. At move three the sequence comes to a halt. Then the cat begins again at move one, restarting the entire sequence.

This 'playing' with prey happens over and over again, which often upsets humans. We call cats cruel for the way they torture wounded mice on our lawns. The cat isn't cruel; it is compulsively performing its predatory sequence, which its brain is designed to do. Unless a cat is distracted by something, the sight of prey means that it has to stalk and pounce.

Sometimes a cat simply can't proceed through its complete hunting programme because the stimulus for triggering the next move simply isn't there. In fact, it is the prey's movement which generally starts off the hunting sequence, making the cat stalk and pounce in the first place.

If a small, shivering mouse, being tortured by a cat, freezes motionless, the cat stops pouncing. Its hunting sequence has been interrupted by the prey's failure to move and trigger the next action.

The same predatory dilemma is seen in play, when our cats watch, stalk and pounce on a cat toy. Most cats ignore a static toy, so we must move it for them. Or they will move it with their paw before they can stalk and pounce on it.

This is play, but for cats that have no opportunity to hunt, play is an important release. Those cats that don't have enough pouncing, grabbing and tearing in their lives may start developing weird behaviours. More of that later.

In the meantime, there is nothing we humans can do to change the cat's mind on hunting. We can take the cat out of the hunting field, but we can't take the hunter out of the cat. Nothing is more rewarding for a cat than hunting. The sequence of actions is innately pleasurable, even if the performance is truncated and there is no fat, juicy mouse at the end.

Understanding the safety instinct

To feel secure, a dog needs a pack, whether human or canine. Yet for an adult cat, security doesn't come in the shape of a companion, whether feline or human. It comes in the shape of a territory and, in particular, the core territory to which it can retreat in complete safety.

Core territory has hiding places where a cat can sleep undisturbed. It has scratch marks where it can leave a message for itself or others, and it has different kinds of scents put there by the cat itself. Home must smell like home for a cat to feel safe. Outside your cat's core territory is a wider, looser territory that is its hunting and patrolling range. This may overlap with other cats' territories.

Within the home territory and hunting range are latrine areas, where the cat can relieve itself without fear of ambush. These must be in the safe sector of the territory, because a cat that is squatting cannot run away. The smell of these areas is reassurance in itself, and sometimes cats share latrines.

But, just to confuse us humans, defecation and urination are also used to mark territorial boundaries. Marks are usually left by spraying urine upright, rather than squatting, and sometimes by defecating and leaving the droppings in full view. Other territory marks are left by rubbing or by scratching.

Understanding the survival instinct

Any time danger threatens, all animals (including humans) have four options. To remember these, it's easiest to think of them as four words all beginning with the letter 'f': fight, flight, freeze and fiddle about (*i.e.* do something that might take a killer's mind off killing you).

Fighting is costly because, in the wild (where there are no vets), an injured animal can easily die from blood poisoning, even from a small wound. Animals that survive by hunting other animals will starve if they get too hurt to hunt.

Cats are small creatures. They haven't a hope in a fight with anything bigger than themselves. Even with something nearer their own size, like a Jack Russell terrier or a fox, they are likely to come off with very severe injuries. Nor, with their small size, can they hope to bluff it out by a threatening show of force.

So for your cat, turning to fight is a last option. Backed up in a confined space, it will hiss, claw and bite, but its preferred strategy is flight and hide. Most cats aim for flight up something, such as a tree, because they are not good long-distance runners. High places make them feel safe.

Better still, your cat will try to avoid danger in the first place. Most cats are neophobic: very cautious in new places, fearful of new people and new things. The shock of a new territory – for instance, when the humans move house – sends many cats to hide under the bed.

Ignore your cat's basic instincts and you will have a stressed, unhappy cat. Work with those same instincts, and your cat will be happy and relaxed.

HUNTING PAWPOINTS

☙ See or hear prey. Eye prey.

☙ Stalk prey. This can take some time, with the animal slinking, then stopping to look. There is sometimes a final fast run forward.

☙ Pounce on prey and grab. This is usually a grabbing bite, but with big prey, the victim may be held down by a paw with claws out.

☙ Bite prey. This is the killing bite, often at the nape of the neck.

☙ Tear off skin or feathers.

☙ Eat.

Remember this sequence. Your cat's drive to hunt is independent of its need to eat.

Doubtless cats talk and reason with one another.

Izaak Walton

(1593–1683)

2

how to understand
what your cat is saying

Your cat has probably worked out how to ask for food and also how to get you to open a door for it. Some cats even let their owners know when it is time (in the cat's opinion) for bed. A surprising number have mastered the tricky business of waking up their owners for a regular 5 a.m. snack.

All this and they don't even use words!

You, for your part, probably know when your feline friend is feeling miserable. You can recognize an ill cat. You know when your cat is particularly enjoying its meal. You know when you have irritated it.

Yet when it comes to communication, our two species are using foreign languages with each other. We humans primarily use a complicated series of vocal sounds that form words. Tone and pitch of voice vary the meaning. We also use body language as a form of expression.

The communication by scent that is so common among animals is, of course, fairly minimal among us. We can learn very little by giving another human being a good sniff, as we have a very poor sense of smell.

Cats, on the other hand, communicate (at least to humans) primarily by means of body language. Secondarily, they use use scent and tactile contact (see pages 50–1). And thirdly, they use vocal noises (see pages 52–3). Scent messages from cat to cat are well understood. Scent messages from a cat to a human are often ignored or misunderstood.

As well as keener hearing and a better sense of smell, cats have a tactile sense organ: their whiskers. These are used more to receive information than to send it.

The better you understand cat talk, the more you will understand your cat.

How to read body language

When humans use body language to convey messages, the main area of communication is the face, with its smiles, frowns, and tears. Dogs also use facial language; they can wrinkle their brows, smile, hang their tongues out, and their facial expression transmits mood messages recognizable to humans. Cat faces are relatively immobile and are difficult for humans to read correctly. But there are some clear signs.

Understanding ear messages

Ears can convey both fear and aggression, if we can understand them. A relaxed but alert cat has its ears forward and erect. The ears go sideways and downwards in a gesture of appeasement in a frightened cat.

 An aggressive cat keeps its ears erect but swivels them backward. The mouth opens, in order to show the teeth that might bite, as the aggression (and fear) increases. A terrified cat ready to fight puts its ears so far back that they are barely visible. Its teeth are also very much on display.

Understanding eye messages

In cat society, it is not polite to stare. A cat that wishes to avoid aggression will avoid eye contact, often by turning its face to one side. Blinking (or narrowed eyes) is another way cats show politeness.

Eye-to-eye confrontation between two cats shows potential aggression. A cat that retreats with a fixed stare is telling an enemy that, if cornered, it will fight. For this reason, humans should take off spectacles if dealing with a frightened cat. Blinking or looking away is also reassuring.

The cat's fear of glaring eyes may also partly account for the way it goes towards people who dislike cats, as those people tend not to make eye contact with them. Intense watching, but not eye-to-eye staring, is also part of the predatory sequence, and may precede a play pounce on another cat.

Understanding body-posture messages

Most of us humans have learned to recognize the message of alarm and aggression in a cat that has its back arched high, its fur fluffed up and its tail held low. Obviously this is a cat trying to make itself look big and threatening. In order to get across the message of maximum size, the cat will often stand sideways on.

A frightened cat that is hoping not to fight back does just the opposite. It lowers its whole body to the ground to make itself as small as possible. This is a signal to show an aggressor that it doesn't want a fight. Its ears are down and flat.

Human beings normally loom over cats. One way to reassure a frightened cat is to lower one's body into a crouch or even lie flat on one's tummy. This is body language which says 'I mean you no harm.'

Then there is the interesting feline body posture known as the social roll. A cat will lie down, exposing its tummy to another cat. This can be an invitation to play or an appeasement gesture meaning 'Don't hurt me. I'm only little.' A hostile cat looming over a rolling cat usually withdraws.

The social roll can sometimes be used by cats as an attention-seeking device when dealing with humans, who can rarely resist responding to it. Some cats (and they are probably in the minority) then enjoy the tummy tickle that follows.

But be warned: a human who unwisely tries to tickle a cat's tummy may find his or her hands caught in the feline rake, where the cat's hind legs kick and claw at the hand. The tummy is a particularly sensitive spot for most cats.

Understanding tail messages

The tail position of a cat going about its business is horizontal or slightly lowered. There is also a tail-up greeting, where a friendly cat comes towards its companion (human or other friendly cat) with its tail held high, often with slight curve forwards at the very tip. This tail-up greeting is not found in wild cats and may have developed during domestication.

Tail-up is also used during body rubbing (which also has a scent message) as the cat weaves itself in and out around human feet. Normally, a cat rubbing round its human's legs is trying to get attention.

A forward tail tip curve is friendly, but there is also a hostile hello in which the bottom half of the tail is raised outwards, but the main part of the tail is curved down. Before a fight, a hostile cat will pull its tail down to get it out of the way. A crouching, terrified cat has its tail tucked right out of sight. No cat wants to risk damage to its tail.

A cat that is twitching or lashing its tail is usually considering an attack. Tail twitching or lashing usually occurs before the pounce, during the cat's hunting stalk. It also occurs when a cat is contemplating an attack on another cat or a human.

Finally, the tail plays a part in feline sexual signals. A female cat on heat will crouch with its backside raised towards the male, its tail held to one side. Pet cats sometimes do a flirty version of this to their humans. They present their backsides, but with the tail up in the friendly greeting posture rather than held aside in the sexual come-on signal.

Understanding claw and paw messages

Cats keep their claws sheathed and walk on their toes. Claws come out to help run up trees or attack. They are used as a weapon during the predatory pounce. A cat with its paw slightly lifted is ready to cuff you! A human with a hand outstretched may look threatening to a cat.

How cats use touch and smell

Cats also use tactile contact and scent to communicate. Many scent messages need tactile contact to be delivered. Most tactile messages also spread scent, and the scent component may be just as important as the tactile contact.

Although a cat's sense of smell is less keen than a dog's, it is nonetheless better than a human's. When a cat delivers a tactile scent message, most humans receive the tactile message but miss the scent that goes with it. They simply cannot smell well enough to notice the scent.

There are scent glands all over the cat's body – beneath the chin, on the cheek, at the corners of the mouth, each side of the forehead, along the tail and between the cat's toes. These give off a scent that most humans cannot perceive, but one that is easily perceived by another cat. When a cat rubs against another cat, it leaves some of its scent behind. It also picks up the scent of the other cat on its own body, mixing the two scents together.

This mixed scent may be the smell of family or home to a cat. It is very important. We recognize our friends by their faces, but scent is the way a cat identifies friends and foes. A family member that smells 'wrong' may be wrongly identified as an enemy. For instance, a cat that has been to the vet and smells of the hated veterinary surgery may be attacked as a hostile intruder by a cat left at home. It may look the same but it smells wrong.

Grooming also probably plays a part both as a tactile and a scent message. The scent from saliva would be left on the groomed cat's fur. Clearly, grooming between cats is a sign of friendship. Enemies don't groom! So if your cat insists on grooming you, take it as a compliment, if an uncomfortable one!

The only scent messages that get through to the human nose are naturally the strong ones: those delivered by urine or faeces left at a significant site. But cats which pass by these feline messages can read much more from them than we can. They can probably tell the gender of the cat which left them and whether it was looking for a mate. They may also be able to read the time when the message was left.

Not so humans. They get very upset, and sometimes very insulted, by these messages. Yet urine and faeces messages are not meant to offend or insult. Inside the house they are usually a cry for help from a cat which is very worried indeed. Spraying and middening are, to the cat, a solution to a problem. They reassure a worried feline, but they are a problem for humans.

Understanding why your cat scratches

The other problem humans face from cats is scratching. Scratching trees, furniture or carpets leaves both a visual signal and also a smell, since there are scent glands between a cat's toes. A scratch is a message board for another cat passing by.

Cats also scratch in the presence of other cats, and it may simply be an ostentatious display of confidence. When one cat has finished scratching, its companion may then take its place.

Cats that scratch furniture in the presence of their owners have discovered yet another way of getting human attention – if not human approval.

HOW TO READ VOCAL SIGNALS

In human vocal language, each word has a series of meanings, and if you are not sure what a word means, you can always look it up in a dictionary.

There is no dictionary for cat language. Cats have a vocal vocabulary, but it is much less important than body language, and it may not be common to all cats. Your cat has acute hearing – it can hear a mouse's footfall – but it usually only recognizes a small number of human words.

Cats vary in their use of sounds. Some cats greet their humans with a kitten 'chirrup'; others with a 'meow'. There are cats that rarely make any sound at all and cats that will use only one or two of the various sounds to their humans. Siamese and Oriental breeds may meow almost all the time that they are with their human.

Older cats are usually more vocal than younger ones. They have probably learned that humans respond better to sound than to body language or scent marks. Thus, they use the meow more frequently and more loudly than in their early years.

Yet there isn't a fixed meaning to a meow. Individual cats may use a slightly different sounding meow for different occasions or contexts – for example, one meow for food and another one for a request to open the door. The meaning varies with individual cats. There is also a kitten distress meow, a call to the mother cat, used when a kitten is in difficulty.

Using cat language

The key to understanding any new foreign language is experience. An inexperienced cat, which is trying to read us, will be better at reading our body language than our vocal words. Yet an experienced cat can understand some of our words – such as the word 'vet'.

The more experience a cat gains around humans, the more words it knows and the more it uses its voice to get through to us.

Talking to your cat

If you want to communicate better with your cat, you can use some of its own signals. With a frightened cat, be careful to give just sideways glances, not a glare. You can try to become lower than the cat. Let it get up higher onto a table or shelf, while you go down to ground level, flat on your tummy.

Inexperienced humans often spend hours of effort in trying to understand a cat's vocal calls, when it would be better to concentrate on its body language. You have probably learned some of this language already, even if you don't know you have done so. Careful attention to its ears and gestures will give further information.

Finally, you can use scent to make your cat feel secure. By petting it, you are putting the scent from your hands upon your cat's body and taking onto your hand its own body scent, thus mixing the two scents in a message of friendship. This action reassures and calms the cat.

It is now possible to buy an artificial phcromone, Feliway, which will help you leave rubbing-scent messages for your cat on furniture or cat pathways within the household (see pages 105–6).

Touch and smell pawpoints

🐾 **Grooming**

Cats who are friendly groom each other, and some cats groom humans. This is because saliva spreads scent, too.

🐾 **Rubbing to mix scents**

This spreads a scent from the cat's skin glands. Cats rub with their chins, their cheeks, their foreheads, flanks and tails. They rub other cats and humans, mixing their scent with others.

🐾 **Rubbing to mark territory**

Cats rub specific marking points in their territory – against shrubs, walls, doorways and large plants.

🐾 **Scratching**

The scent glands between a cat's toes leave a smell on the scratched area. Scratching is also a visual signal.

❧ Spraying

Entire tom cats spray, but so, at times, do neutered males and females. The cat stands at full height, arches its back, and squirts a jet of urine. The body posture shows that this is territorial marking.

❧ Middening

The cat uses faeces to send a message as well as to mark territory. The faeces are left uncovered as a visual as well as scent signal. Faeces are often left along walkways at the edge of territory.

❧ Squat marking

Just to confuse their humans, cats will occasionally mark territory by urinating when squatting. This marking can only be distinguished from ordinary urination by its location. It is said that the urine smells more pungent than ordinary urine.

Talking pawpoints

❧ Chirrup

This is a little chirrup or trill used as a greeting between cats and their kittens, sometimes to humans.

❧ Purr

Used when nursing kittens or as a response to tactile contact. It can be switched on by the physical nearness of familiar humans or by familiar pleasant places. Some cats purr almost silently, creating more of a vibration than a sound.

❧ Meow

An attention-seeking noise which varies in length. The meaning varies with context. Some cats are almost silent. Older cats meow more than younger ones – probably because they know their humans take more notice of sound than body language. Orientals use long meows frequently.

🐾 Growl
A warning sign of aggression. Cats that growl are seriously angry and may bite!

🐾 Yowl
On a rising note, a warning sound.

🐾 Hiss
A defensive sound, meaning 'back off'.

🐾 Spit
A more violently defensive sound.

🐾 Chatter
This is an involuntary excited predatory noise, made when a cat is watching prey but cannot get at it.

🐾 Caterwauling and sexual calls
Neutered and spayed cats don't need or use them – for obvious reasons.

A cat is more intelligent than people believe,
and can be taught any crime.
MARK TWAIN
(1835–1910)

how to help
your cat learn

From the moment you bring home a new kitten, you are teaching it how to behave, whether you know that or not. And although you won't realize it, your kitten is teaching you how to behave, too.

The idea that cats can't learn is, frankly, ridiculous. Every single scientific experiment has shown that cats are remarkably quick learners – *if* they are motivated to do so. Problems only occur when the proposed lesson is unsuited to their nature.

For instance, it is easy to teach a pointer to point at a sitting bird. Not only does the dog have the pointing instinct, but it is also happy to follow men about.

It would be extremely difficult to teach a cat to point, for many reasons. A cat would be frightened at being taken into a strange territory. It would also be terrified by the noises of guns, and it would be scared by the presence of strange human beings.

Unlike dogs, cats are not much reassured by the presence of their owners.

Making your kitten bomb-proof

Well before it even arrives at its new home, your kitten has learned several lessons. Indeed, the behaviour of your adult cat is defined by its experiences as a kitten.

The single most important lesson that your pet cat needs is how to bond with human beings. If it doesn't learn this as a kitten, it may never learn it for the rest of its life. It will always be wary around human beings and will grow up as a feral cat. Most feral cats can't be handled. They will avoid contact with humans, except for cautious approaches if food is left down regularly.

There is a small window of opportunity in kittenhood when a cat can learn that humans are friends. Tiny kittens do not know fear. You can handle them and cuddle them much more easily than older cats.

For the first few weeks they are just little care-eliciting babies. They don't run; if anything, kittens purposefully approach you. Their demeanour, their tiny mews, are nature's way of inducing their mothers, or even their humans, to look after them.

This fear-free window is called the sensitive period and it falls between the second and seventh week of kitten life. The process of accepting a different species as a friend is often called 'socialization'. This has to happen before kittens get the fear instinct, which kicks in around the eighth week and grows stronger until the fifteenth week.

Handling your kitten with care

During the five-week period before it knows fear, your kitten needs to be handled by at least four different humans, preferably including men, women and also children. The more handling your kitten has had, the friendlier it will be in later life to humans. It also needs to get used to the smell of humans, since smell is important for the feline identification of friend or foe.

If it is to be adopted into a home with a dog, your kitten also needs to meet a friendly dog during this period. And if it is going to be happy in a home with lots of other cats, it needs to meet other adult cats, not just its mother, during its kittenhood. It needs to learn how to handle a social life! An only kitten, brought up in isolation with just its mother, may become a bit of a loner and will be happier as a single pet.

During this sensitive period, your kitten also needs to get used to the host of human noises, household smells and daily sounds and sights of an ordinary human home. It will learn that it need not be frightened by the noises of the washing machine, the telephone, the radio and the television.

The ideal home for a kitten is a noisy household with children, friends who visit, a calm, loving dog, and one or two other cats. Growing up in this atmosphere will mean your kitten is used to, and not frightened by, most domestic activities.

The worst upbringing for a pet cat is to be born in the wild. Kittens that are rescued off the street need a lot of handling as early as possible by their rescuers in order to overcome their fear of humans. Rescuers who don't realize this may hand out kittens for adoption that will grow up to be wild animals. While these can sometimes be tamed by endless human patience, they rarely make easy pets.

The other bad upbringing is that of a pedigree kitten reared in a cat chalet, a shed or a quiet spare room. Kitten farms, where kittens are produced cheaply en masse for sale to pet shops or via small ads, produce physically sick and emotionally stunted kittens. These are the kittens often found in pet shops. Good breeders never sell their stock to shops, so any kittens on sale will come from a relatively unscrupulous person.

Even some pedigree breeders who love and cherish their cats simply don't understand the importance of exposing their kittens at an early age to human life in all its forms. They think a stress-free environment is good for kittens. The reverse is true. Kittens need to be exposed to stress: the sounds, smells and activities of an ordinary human home.

When buying a kitten, try to check if there are cat chalets at the bottom of the garden. Some breeders will show the buyer their kittens in the house, but then stick them back into the shed or chalet when the would-be buyer has left. These kittens will have difficulty adapting to a human home.

Posh pedigrees alone do little for a kitten. Only a good education with lots of handling makes for a happy pet.

How to nurture your kitten

Your kitten learns a lot from its mother in the first few weeks of its life. At four weeks, it starts eating solid food and is taught what it should eat. Researchers have discovered that if a mother cat has been trained to eat bananas, her kittens learn to enjoy bananas, too. So a kitten that has been brought up on only one type of food will prefer that type in later life. A kitten that has been offered a variety of different foods will be less fussy about what it eats as an adult.

Understanding the hunting instinct

Hunting is also picked up by watching mum. A mother cat starts bringing her kittens dead prey when they are about four weeks old. Later she brings in live prey and helps them hunt it down. So a kitten that is fed on birds by its mother will prefer to hunt birds.

The hunting instinct is so strong, however, that kittens which have never come across living prey can still learn to hunt, even late in life. A pampered pedigree cat, brought up on tinned food all its life, will be a poor hunter to start with, but in time it will learn to catch mice. The basic instinct is that powerful.

You cannot normally train a cat to stop hunting living prey. All you can do is shut the cat away, depriving it of the chance to exercise its most powerful natural instinct. An indoor life is not the life for which most cats were designed.

Litter training and weaning

Litter preferences also start early. Kittens begin to use litter at around the age of five weeks. If they are placed on litter, they will begin to dig it. They get used to the smell and the feel of whatever is in the litter tray. If your kitten was originally introduced to wood chips, it will probably prefer wood chips as litter when it is a cat.

Then there is the weaning experience. As kittens eat more solid food, they begin to grow teeth, and naturally their mother is less keen to be suckled. When they are about seven weeks old, she will begin to refuse them her nipples. By being refused milk, the kittens learn to eat solid food.

Understanding frustration

Kittens also learn another very important lesson at this time. As they are refused their mother's nipples, they experience times of frustration when they can't get what they want. The mother leaves them or lies down, hiding her tummy. She starts refusing their overtures. They are left to cope without her help. This experience of frustration is important as it will enable them to tolerate other frustrating experiences later in life without losing their emotional cool.

Bottle-fed kittens sometimes miss out on this frustration experience. Even if the bottle is withdrawn, soft food is immediately offered in its place. They never experience a refusal and may grow into cats that cannot tolerate frustration. These cats use their claws on humans to get their own way.

Although the most important lessons take place before the age of eight weeks, cats can learn them after that time. It will just take longer for the lessons to be learned, and they may be learned less thoroughly. It is therefore important to influence your new kitten's behaviour as early as possible.

However, you cannot work wonders. Cats, like humans, are influenced not just by their education but also by their genes. Some cats are naturally more aloof than others. You can make an aloof cat into a cat that is confident around humans, but you cannot make it into a cat that enjoys cuddles.

Teaching your kitten

Some behaviour can be trained into a cat early on. If you have two homes – a town flat and a weekend country cottage – you may want a cat that is not frightened by car travel. In this case, the best plan would be to get a kitten as near the age of eight weeks as possible and accustom it to being driven in a car from the beginning. If you explain this, a rescue shelter be able to help.

But many pedigree breeders will not let a kitten go to its new home until it is fourteen weeks old. You might therefore ask the breeder if he or she will drive it around in the first few weeks of its life. If the breeder refuses, you will just have to accustom it to car travel as soon as possible. And, to make sure that it becomes accustomed, it would be worth driving it around a little every day for the first two or three weeks.

The experience should be made as pleasant as possible. Small items of particularly delicious food should be offered when the kitten is first put in its travelling box. The box can also be sprayed with Feliway, the artificial scent which is used to promote relaxation in cats (see pages 105-6).

The same procedure is used for a cat being taught to wear a leash. In this case, put the harness on before meals. Only when the cat is completely used to being in the harness should it be taken out with it – first into safe places, then slowly into unfamiliar ones.

Nail-clipping, teeth-cleaning, and intensive grooming for long-haired cats should be started as early as possible and performed frequently. The younger your kitten, the quicker it will become accustomed to these activities. Each experience should be made pleasant by using good food treats.

Eliminating bad behaviour

You can also train out bad behaviour. One frequent mistake is to encourage your kitten to play rough games with humans. It is so sweet to see it pouncing with its claws out or even inflicting a tiny bite. The wound is so small that it hardly seems to matter at all.

But when your cat is an adult and it continues the same rough games, the pain can be quite intense. You may mistakenly punish the cat and find that punishment increases its aggression. So from the earliest days, it is important that games using claws or teeth are not allowed. The game should stop immediately at the first sign of these.

Promoting good behaviour

Many humans mistakenly believe that the best way to get rid of bad behaviour must be via punishment. Cats won't stick around for punishment. Pain or fear will poison your relationship with your cat, and the cat is unlikely to know why pain is being inflicted.

Remember, cats avoid danger whenever possible before it happens, so rather than risk punishment from you, your cat may just decide you are not a safe person to be near. It may feel that its home is not a safe place to live in and respond by scent-marking with urine or faeces. One really bad experience with you, and your cat could leave home in order to find a core territory without what it considers to be abusive human behaviour.

Your cat (like all animals) will respond much better to rewards for good behaviour. But to do this, you have to learn what is rewarding for your individual cat. What *you* think is rewarding is not necessarily what your cat thinks. Petting or tactile contact is very important to us, but it is usually less rewarding to a cat.

Nor are cats, like dogs, anxious for our approval; verbal praise will not be very motivating. Food, attention and games are probably good rewards, and individual cats may respond best to just one or two of these.

Using non-rewards

There is an alternative to punishment. This system of non-reward, as the behaviour experts like to call it, is a powerful tool for changing animal behaviour. It is not punishment, as no pain is inflicted: only disappointment. If a cat is expecting a titbit or some attention and does not get it, it will learn to avoid the behaviour that did not get the expected reward.

Take, for example, the constant yowl of a cat such as a Siamese. Normally, humans respond to the cries in several ways. They pick up the cat, they talk back to the cat, or they may even shout a rebuke at the cat. All these responses are human attention, and for an attention-seeking cat, even a rebuke is a reward.

Breaking the attention-seeking cycle

Cries will be magically reduced if the human never, ever gives that attention when a cat is yowling. Instead, the human pays attention to the cat only when it is silent. Thus, the human is using a reward of attention for silence and using a non-reward of ignoring the cat for unwanted yowling.

In the same way, if a rough game is halted immediately, the cat will learn to stop the clawing that ended the game. Continuing the game would be a reward; ending the game is a non-reward. Thus games with sheathed claws can be encouraged by the continuance of the game: a reward. Games with claws unsheathed are discouraged by ending the game: a non-reward.

Thinking like your cat

Even armed with this knowledge, changing cat behaviour is difficult. The main problem lies in the fact that we humans find it difficult to think like cats. We don't time our rewards or non-rewards correctly. We think a cat understands us far better than it does.

For instance, people often say 'Bad cat!' in a threatening tone of voice to a cat that is scratching the furniture. From the human point of view, this is a punishment. But a confident cat may well think of the rebuke as a reward; it has successfully got its owner's attention. It stops scratching temporarily because now it has achieved its aim: human attention. But it will scratch again when it wants its human to notice it again.

Training pawpoints

🐾 Punishment

Never use physical or verbal punishment. Use non-rewards instead.

🐾 Rewards

Use those the individual cat desires. Not all cats are motivated by the same things.

🐾 Avoid force

Instead, set up a situation so that your cat does what you want, then reward it.

🐾 Timing

Your cat must be rewarded exactly at the time it performs the desired behaviour. Rewards that come too late are ineffective.

🐾 Read a book

Training by reward can be adapted to cats. Clicker training solves timing difficulties.

Reward pawpoints

🐾 Food

The better the food, the greater the reward. Prawns motivate behaviour much more than bits of a cat's normal diet.

🐾 Attention

Most pet cats enjoy human attention. If you want to encourage behaviour, respond by giving attention.

🐾 Games

The predatory sequence of eye, stalk and pounce is innately rewarding to all cats.

🐾 Discouragements and non-rewards

Refuse to give food when the cat is expecting it. Refuse all attention: deny all eye contact, stay silent, turn the whole body away or walk out of the room. Or simply stop playing the game.

The cat is truly an aristocrat in type and origin.
ALEXANDRE DUMAS
(1802–1870)

4

how to look after
your pedigree cat

Pedigrees benefit humans, not cats. From your cat's point of view, being pure-bred or having champions in its bloodlines has no value at all. Cat shows are run by humans for humans, not for cats. Cats don't care if they win or lose, and every single cat in a cat show would much prefer to be hunting a mouse rather than sitting in a boring cage being stared at by passers-by. Your pedigree cat will always be happiest treated as a proper cat, not as an object on show.

All cats were just cats until artist Harrison Weir held the first big cat show at Crystal Palace, London, in 1871. He hoped that cat shows would improve the status of cats, which, at that time, were treated far less well than dogs. If shows really did achieve a higher status for cats, then this is one real benefit.

Yet the business of showing has also cost individual cats dearly. Many have lost their freedom to roam and their freedom to hunt. They still have their freedom to reproduce, unlike many pet neutered cats, but this involves heavy restrictions for stud cats, usually imprisoned in cat chalets rather than in a household because of their habit of spraying.

Understanding your cat's genetic legacy

Worse still, once an animal has been declared a pedigree, it joins a highly restricted gene pool. A Persian can only mate with a Persian, or a Burmese with a Burmese. Some breeds were started with only a few dozen foundation animals, so the gene pool was incredibly small at the beginning of the breed. A small gene pool means that animals have genes in common with those with whom they mate.

Recessive genes for a disorder can be carried by an apparently healthy cat. If that cat mates with a cat free from the gene, the disorder never shows up. But if it mates with a cat that is also a carrier, the gene will become dominant, transmitting what are now noticeable inherited disorders to the kittens.

Any weaknesses or inherited disorders will become more and more evident in successive generations as the artificially restricted gene pool excludes new genes (see page 88).

It gets worse. The business of showing cats successfully restricts the gene pool even further. Successful breeders often 'line-breed'. This means that they will mate son to mother or cousin to cousin in order to fix the look that has led to prizes in the show ring. The kittens are thus further inbred.

Even without any deliberate line-breeding, success in the show world has a tendency to reduce the gene pool further. A stud cat that wins in a major show will be chosen to mate with more females than a less successful stud. Thus, his genes will predominate in the kittens sired for the next few years.

This wouldn't matter so much if cat shows chose the healthiest and most robust animals as their champions – but they don't. They choose the prettiest. Energy, fitness and the ability to mouse are not awarded prizes. Winners don't have to function well; they just have to look good.

Judges can often make things worse by choosing the cat that is the 'most' Persian or the 'most' Siamese. They look for what is called 'type'. In 1871, Persian cats had long hair and noses that did not look much unlike ordinary cats. Now they have snub noses like pug dogs, and there is even a strain called Ultra Persians whose noses are so smashed back against their faces that they have severe breathing difficulties.

Similarly, Siamese used to look more or less like ordinary cats, except for being a little lighter in build. Now they have been bred to be ultra-thin animals with long, tapering, wedge-shaped heads (see page 89).

How to read pedigree instincts

Pedigree cats behave like cats – if they get the chance. Their hunting instinct is still there. Persians have a reputation for being poor hunters, but this probably arises from the fact so many are kept as indoor cats with no chance of practising their skills. Max, a Persian cat that lived in a canal boat with his family with free access to the bank, once brought home seven mice in one evening, having eaten one or two on the bank beforehand. He regularly caught young rabbits, shrews, voles, mice, frogs, toads and even rats – just like any non-pedigree cat.

Yet most Persians and exotic cats seem to be relatively lethargic. One reason may be that they have been bred for placidity in the show ring. The other reason why they may differ from ordinary moggies in their behaviour is simply because they cannot breathe properly. Cats with the extreme flat face may not be able to draw in enough oxygen to their lungs, so they cannot help but be lethargic.

There is one real behaviour difference between Siamese and ordinary moggies. The Siamese, and the breeds developed from them, have a tendency to be more vocal than ordinary cats. Those that love the breed say that they are 'talkative'. Those that find the constant meowing difficult consider them over-demanding. Siamese may also be far more prone to the strange disorder of wool-sucking or eating strange substances. See 'Eating disorders', page 126.

Understanding other breeds

Other breed differences are less clear. Burmese, for instance, may seem particularly sensitive and anxious, but this apparent breed difference could perhaps arise simply because cat breeders do not understand how to rear pet kittens.

Some breeders fail to grasp the importance of proper kitten socialization before the age of eight weeks. Their kittens may be bred in a cat chalet or quiet room and handled only by the breeder rather than by several other people. Pedigree cat people like the idea of giving extra-special care to their animals – not realizing that a rough-and-tumble regime is far better for the future pet. The kittens produced under this regime will always be relatively fearful and nervous adult cats. Thus, what appears to be a breed behaviour difference is simply the result of a bad upbringing.

Recognizing the role of fur

Hair makes quite an obvious difference to behaviour. The Sphynx cat, a hairless breed, always seeks out warm surfaces and is happy in, rather than on, the bed with its owner. Rex cats, which lack the outer layer of hair, will also need more warmth.

Conversely, all long-haired cats, whether pedigree or not, will be far less likely to be lap cats. Wearing a thick coat, even in a centrally heated house, they seek out cool places rather than the warmth of body contact with their owner. Long-haired and semi-long-haired cats are more likely to be found stretched out in an attempt to lose heat, rather than curled up in an attempt to preserve warmth.

They also require regular brushing – daily for a Persian or long-haired cat and every other day for a semi-long-haired cat – to get rid of loose hair. This loose hair is otherwise swallowed by the cat when it grooms itself. Hairballs form in its stomach, blocking the gut and causing a lack of appetite and constipation. It may also vomit up hairballs.

Ungroomed long-haired cats have fur that begins to mat very quickly. The mats tighten, pulling at the roots of the fur, and soon the skin under the mat becomes sore. Once the mats have been allowed to form, brushing becomes painful; as soon as a cat sees the grooming tools, it runs away. For ways to groom a fearful cat, see pages 90–1.

How your indoor cat behaves

The other behaviour difference between pedigree and non-pedigree cats has nothing to do with their shape or breed. It is just that pedigree cat owners are more likely to keep their cats indoors all the time, denying them access to the great outdoors. Indeed, some breeders will only sell kittens if these are to be kept indoors all their lives.

An indoor cat is protected from disease and will lead a longer and healthier life than a cat that is allowed out of doors. This physical health, however, comes at the cost to its psychological health. If your cat is a solitary indoor cat without daytime human companionship, it will probably be bored. It is deprived of opportunities to fulfil its hunting instinct, and is therefore more likely to develop behaviour problems.

You can do a great deal, however, to help your pedigree or indoor cat lead a better life indoors.

Installing scratching posts

Provide these. Spray with catnip spray, if your cat needs encouragement and if it is sensitive to catnip. Consider buying a post with a carpet-lined hidey hole higher up. This will give your cat a chance to express its climbing skills.

Playing

A cat needs to work off predatory instincts in play. Get a fishing-rod toy. Throw balls of paper or kitchen foil. In the wild, a cat would hunt about ten mice a day, so give your cat thirty pounces every day.

Providing toys

You can hang ropes from the ceiling; provide cardboard boxes with holes to get into, and plenty of newspapers to claw. In addition, put dry food into puzzle feeders for a more challenging mealtime.

Good shop toys include crinkle bags, toy fur-covered mice, etc. Toys that are easy to move around are best. Be sure to change the toys daily.

Providing viewpoints

Make sure your cat can look out of the window and see other living things. Eyeing prey is the first part of the predatory sequence. Put a bird feeder up for it to look at. You can even buy special feeders that stick to the glass.

Provide sitting places, on ledges and shelves at the window with a view of passers-by, such as dogs, wildlife or other cats.

Giving regular meals

Offer food four times a day, if possible. If cats were in the wild, they would have to stalk and hunt for food. Get rid of the food bowl. Hide dry food around the house so that your cat has to hunt for it. Throw pieces of food so the cat has to chase them – this is useful exercise.

Training your cat

Clicker training or ordinary tricks will fire the reward chemistry in your cat's brain. Clicker-trained cats will often go through a whole session of little games, purring non-stop. Don't train for an audience, though; just do it for good fun for both of you.

Construct an agility course; a book on clicker-training will explain how it's done. Almost anything is better than a cat which has nothing to do.

PROBLEM PAWPOINTS

🐾 **Polycystic kidney disease, or PKD**
This ailment is a high risk in Persians and Exotics, and a medium risk in several other breeds. Cats die early with kidney disease. Ultra-sound tests to rule out PKD are now available for breeders. Never buy from a breeder with untested stock.

🐾 **Gangliosidosis, or GM1 and GM2**
An enzyme deficiency in Korat cats and American Siamese. A test is now available. Do not buy untested stock.

🐾 **Heart disease**
Possibly inherited in American Maine Coon and American Short-hair cats and more frequent (though maybe not inherited) in flat-faced cats.

These inherited disorders may also be transmitted to first-generation cross cats.

🐾 **Extreme flat face in Persian and Exotic cats**
The extremely flat face produces difficulties with breathing, tear-duct problems, and even jaw and teeth deformations. Symptoms may include snoring, the inability to take exercise because of a lack of oxygen, or continually watering eyes. In the worst cases, the cat's food must be liquidized. Ignore championships in the pedigree and avoid abnormalities in the mother.

🐾 **Excessive fur in long-hair breeds**
Too much fur on any cat means more hairballs. Mats form if not groomed daily.

🐾 **Ultra-slim body in Siamese**
Some individuals squint. Tail kinks look bad but do not affect cat welfare.

🐾 **Deafness**
Commonest in white cats with blue eyes.

GROOMING PAWPOINTS

😺 Deal with any existing mats.

😺 Lay in some very, very tasty treats. Allow a week or two – or even longer – for each stage. Patience is the key here.

😺 Accustom the cat to being touched by a non-grooming tool such as a spoon while holding a treat. Do this for several days.

😺 Then, over several days, start moving the tool through the hair. Pretend to groom, and treat accordingly.

😺 Holding the treat in the left hand, let the cat nibble it while you brush its back with a soft brush.

😺 Only when the cat fully accepts this brushing, proceed to brushing the neck ruff.

🐾 Hold the treat at ground level so the cat almost has to lie down to reach it. Say 'Lie down' while you do this. When the cat lies down, give the treat.

🐾 When this response is established, hold the treat and brush a little along the side of the body before giving the cat the treat.

🐾 The next stage involves holding the treat so that the cat has to lie on its back in order to nibble it. Then, brush gently around the tail for a few moments, while it is still nibbling. Most cats will respond by moving their back paws nearer the head, thus exposing their tail area.

🐾 Once an ordinary brush has been accepted by your cat, you can begin using a slicker metal brush as well.

I... am forced to entertain myself as well as I can with my little dog and cat. They both of them sit by my fire every night.
SIR RICHARD STEELE
(1672–1729)

5

how to protect your cat's territorial rights

Humans, with all the arrogance of a supposedly superior species (tell that to your cat!), expect domestic animals to fit into their lifestyles. They bring cats into their homes and expect them to follow a human timetable and human rules.

The human decides whether the cat shall reproduce; what, how much and when the cat will eat; when, where and how long the pet will sleep; what, if any, recreation it is allowed; and when and where it will be allowed to urinate and defecate.

Worse still, the human lays down these rules but is abysmally bad at making them clear to the feline, because humans simply don't think like cats.

Playing by feline rules

From the beginning in your human-cat relationship, your cat is acting under a wholly different set of ideas to yours. It is living by cat rules. What seems like common sense to you looks like idiocy to your cat.

And what seems like perversity to you is often good behaviour to your cats.

Of course, cats will try to fit into your world. They are adaptable creatures and have managed to live alongside us for about 6,000 years in reasonable harmony. But this adaptability doesn't alter your cat's basic reactions. In other words, your cat won't change itself to suit you.

So, if the relationship isn't working out, it will be you (rather than your cat) who will have to change. And to know what to do, you must learn cat rules. If possible, you must learn to think like a cat and understand the world through your cat's eyes.

The biggest difference between humans and cats has to do with how they think of territory. A house, which is a happy home to its human occupant, may not be a happy home to a cat.

How your cat sees territory

For most humans, home has clear, fixed boundaries, and we mark these boundaries with solid walls. If we live in a flat, indoors is home and humans don't enter unless we let them. We control the space completely.

If we live in a house with a garden, we have slightly different boundaries, marked not just by walls but also by fences, hedges or wire netting. In open-plan estates, only a small line of shrubs marks the boundaries, but the garden is definitely our space. We control the garden boundaries, and other humans don't enter unless we ask them in. We keep out of theirs.

Your cat, however, doesn't recognize these boundaries at all. For a cat, there is a core home territory and a home range for hunting. A cat that spends some time out of doors usually recognizes indoors as its core home territory – more or less. But it never actually recognizes that physical boundaries, such as walls or doors, mark territories. These are obviously obstacles for all cats, but they do not necessarily stand for fixed boundaries to them.

This may be why cats make their humans into door-keepers, asking to be let out only to insist on being let in again a number of times. They don't recognize the human meaning of doors, seeing them merely as inconvenient obstacles. Going in and out reassures them that the outside hunting range is still open to them.

Interpreting the garden
The most obvious examples of the territorial difference between you and your cat are the walls or hedges of your garden. You stay inside the walls and hedges, even though you could climb over them into your next-door neighbour's garden space. Your cat often pays no attention to them and may

treat your neighbour's garden as part of its hunting range, unless frightened out of it.

Your cat also has a different attitude to roads. You see a road as a pathway and also as a barrier. You take care in crossing it. Your cat probably doesn't see the road as a pathway at all, and it has only a vague sense of it as a barrier. Passing cars will make it pause before crossing, but it has no sense of the potential danger. If your cat lives near a main road, it will not hesitate to cross it to get to an attractive hunting ground at the other side. It simply doesn't recognize traffic danger. At night, when its eyes are dazzled by headlights, this could cost it its life. It has its own pathways, which may well not coincide with ours.

Your cat has a 'smell map' of its territory, defined by scent markings left by itself: chin-rubbing places and urine-spraying places. It may avoid the places where a frightening local cat sprays, recognizing these spray marks as feline notices which say things with the same boldness as graffiti, such as 'Watch out! – Tabby is here'. At other spray sites it will recognize messages left by more than one cat, marking areas where several cats share territory. It may add its own mark to the existing ones. These areas are more like a feline village green, where several cats can legitimately enjoy the area in common, though perhaps at different times.

Your cat may even discover some spray messages (perhaps from cats in season) that invite other cats to come up and see them sometime! Because we don't smell well, we can't be sure of their meanings.

Finally, your cat will also recognize, visually and by scent, scratch marks within its territory. It may add its own. They may mean 'Tabby was here' or 'Look at me: I scratch higher!'

Securing home territory

All these marks have one thing in common: the smell is reassuring to the cat that makes it. When a cat rubs or sprays or scratches, it feels better. The smell is reassuring, like the smell of home.

A happy cat needs a safe home territory. It can usually live happily enough with a hunting range which overlaps with other cats – after all, pet cats don't need to hunt for food. But its core territory, where it sleeps, must be safe from intruding strangers, whether human or animal.

This core territory has to smell right – it must smell of the cat itself. So your cat will go around its home, making scent marks that are invisible to humans, rubbing its chin and its cheek on various items in the house. A house is not a home until it smells of home. Only then can your cat feel relaxed.

Each time it rubs against a chair or a table leg, it leaves its own scent and picks up the scent of the household item. The home scent is a mixture of smells: your cat itself, household furniture, other living beings in the house. Where your cat leaves invisible rubbing messages, it will not need to do any other scent markings, so it will not need to spray or leave a faeces message where it has rubbed.

Understanding the need to scratch

Although usually your cat will not need to scent mark its home by spraying, it will do so by scratching as well as rubbing. Your cat stands on its back legs at full height and rakes its legs down a vertical surface, or does a horizontal scratch across a carpet.

Scratching conditions its claws, but it also conveys a message, visual and scented, to other cats. This scratching often occurs in front of a familiar cat companion or a familiar human and is a 'Look at me' message. Certainly, cats that scratch in front of humans often do so in order to get human attention – even if the attention is of the 'Stop doing that' variety. Your cat probably knows that if it starts scratching the furniture, you will immediately look at it and say something rude. As an attention-seeking device, scratching works well!

Your cat has to mix its scent with other family members. Remember, cat rules identify family mainly by scent, not sight. Anybody who doesn't smell like family is not welcome in its home territory. So your cat rubs up against you in a friendly way, partly to get your attention and partly to mix its scent.

Rubbing along together

When you pet your cat, you are following proper cat behaviour rules. By stroking your cat, you are mixing your two scents. Your hand now smells of the cat and the cat now smells of your hand. From the cat's point of view, petting means that you are doing a friendly family scent rub! You are, without realizing it, behaving like a cat should, and you are strengthening the bond between you.

Cats will also rub against household dogs. If your cat met a family dog when it was a kitten, it will have no difficulty adapting to a dog in the household. Likewise, a dog that has met cats when it was a puppy will be relaxed around cats in the home. Both seem able to communicate, learning enough of each other's body language to get along.

Difficulties between dogs and cats arise only when a cat that has never known dogs is forced to live with one. The worst-possible scenario for your cat will occur if it has to live with a dog that has been taught to chase cats. A sensible cat, faced with ever-present danger in its core territory, will usually leave home.

If you take up with a new partner who comes with dogs or other cats, you may have to think about rehoming your existing cat. Or, of course, you could rehome the partner!

How to play happy families

Not all cats enjoy living with other cats. Cats are not pack animals like dogs. A kitten that never met any other cats except for its mother and siblings may not be keen in later life to live in a feline family with other cats.

If your cat has spent its first adult months as a solitary pet in a household, it will find adapting to other cats very difficult indeed. Even if, as a kitten, your cat was brought up to get along with other cats, it may have difficulty when a new cat is introduced into your home. It is unlikely to greet the newcomer with anything other than hostility.

Understanding the importance of scent

Any new cat smells like a foe, not a friend. It hasn't yet acquired the home smell of your house, so your cat will automatically treat it as an intruder. Until it acquires the right home-smell mixture, it will never be accepted by your existing cat. This can take several weeks.

Indeed, if your existing cat has a solitary nature, it may never truly like its new companion. It will share its home territory with the newcomer, but their relationship will be one of armed neutrality, not friendship.

Scent can also sometimes lead to fights between cats that have hitherto been friends. A sudden antagonism may occur if one of your cats has returned home from time spent in another household or in the vet's surgery. It comes home smelling of the vet – a smell that is extremely upsetting and badly wrong to the first cat. As a result, its companion attacks it as if it were a strange intruder.

Although, as a human, you will never be able to fully understand the importance of smell messages, you can now get help from the vet. Vets sell a product called Feliway, which is an artificial scent made to smell like the rubbing scent of a cat. Most humans can't detect the smell, but cats can, and it makes most of them feel more relaxed. It comes either in spray form or as a diffuser that is plugged into the mains.

So if you want to help your cat get used to a new feline companion, you can plug a Feliway Diffuser into the room where both cats spend most of their time. The relaxing scent will last about a month and will reduce the tension between them. Or you can use the Feliway spray daily around the household pathways at cat chin height.

There is also a similar product called Felifriend that is used by vets and cat workers to make their hands smell friendly to cats. If you spray this on your own hands and then stroke both cats, this, too, may help to promote harmony between them. You can add to the family scent mix by swapping the cats' bedding so that the two cats begin to smell of each other.

There is a cheaper alternative to Feliway, which is useful for cats that do not respond to the product. Its only disadvantage is that it requires you to have the kind of cat which enjoys having its cheek and chin rubbed.

Using a small piece of white cloth, such as a handkerchief, rub this on your cat's cheek and chin. Then, using the same cloth, do the same to the new cat, transferring your existing cat's scent to the newcomer. Next, transfer the new cat's scent back to your existing cat. Do this twice daily for at least two weeks. This will only work if both cats are relaxed about the procedure. If your rubbing cheek and chin with a handkerchief upsets either cat, it will only make things worse between them. If so, try the same trick with fingers only.

Providing plenty of everything

In order to maximize harmony between cats, it is important to make sure that there are more than enough beds, food bowls and litter trays. There should be one litter tray for each cat and one extra – just in case. This is particularly important if your cat is being harassed by one of its feline companions, which may be ambushing it on its way to or from the litter tray.

Ensuring security in the litter tray

A sense of security when using the litter tray is essential to a cat's feeling of happiness within its core home territory. Cats are usually taught their toilet arrangements by their mother. Most pet cats will be familiar with a particular kind of cat litter. Kittens that have started life out of doors may be used to soil or sand, as may stray adult cats that have lived rough for a long time.

The type of litter is important, because the feel of it under the paws will trigger your cat to use it. It's just like a human being that wants to go, but it is being seated on the loo seat that allows the release of the urge. A cat that has been used to soil will not be happy with commercial litter. So, when getting a new cat or a new kitten, it is important to find out what kind of litter it is used to.

If you ever want to change to a different type, do this slowly, handful by handful, over several weeks. On the whole, cats prefer expensive, fine-grained litter to coarse ones. Heavy wood litters or light litters made from recycled newspapers are unpopular with some cats. It is essential that your cat is happy with its litter tray. An unhappy cat will go outside the tray, so it is in your interests to make it happy!

Not only does your cat need familiar litter, it also needs a safe place for the litter tray. Cats do not like to use a litter tray in their feeding or sleeping areas, so the litter tray must be some distance from the food bowl and the bed.

It should also be in a relatively secluded area, and not in a place where humans or other pets are often walking by. Cats feel vulnerable when they are using the tray. A covered tray can help. Experiment with a cardboard box with a hole cut in it before buying a covered one – just in case your cat is the rare animal that prefers an open tray.

Your cat will also prefer clean litter. It does not like having to dig through soiled litter, so clean the tray at least twice a day. If you can't do this, set up a second tray for each cat so that no tray gets too dirty. Be generous with litter. Your cat may like a good dig.

Dealing with the litter tray

Do not use a deodorant litter or a spray-on deodorant; this makes the litter tray smell wrong to some cats. Your cat likes a clean tray that still smells ever so slightly like a latrine. A sensitive cat sometimes refuses to use a litter tray that has been used by its companion cat, so add extra trays. Or it may refuse to use the same tray for both urination and defecation. If so, install two trays – one for one, another for the other.

If a cat has a bad experience while it is on the litter tray, it may take against the tray itself. Bad experiences include abdominal pain while using the tray, cystitis pain, being ambushed while on the tray by another cat, fear of a sudden loud noise, or fear because of some other unexpected occurrence. The cat usually blames the tray for this! The only answer is to buy a new tray.

Your cat may also stop using the litter tray if you change the position of it. If this happens, put the tray back to its original position and move it about six inches a day towards the new position.

Occasionally, your cat's ability to use the litter tray may appear to break down altogether. Your cat soils the house all over the place and does not respond to better toilet arrangements. In this case, always check with the vet in case the animal is ill. If not, it may help to call in a pet behaviour counsellor, via your vet, who can provide some expert advice after seeing you, the cat and the household arrangements.

If all this seems like too much trouble, then remember: it is in your interests to keep your cat happy – and therefore house-trained.

How to make a tough decision

No cat should live in constant fear and intimidation of other cats or dogs. For its own sake, a victim cat needs a new home. Cats with outdoor access will often just leave home altogether or start living in the garden. It is kinder to find them a new home, perhaps as a single cat. The following signs may indicate that it is time to re-home.

- The cat needs veterinary treatment for bitten ears, skin, or abscesses after bites.

- The cat is afraid to enter the house and spends most of its time out of doors.

- The cat spends most of its time in hiding.

- The cat is no longer grooming itself.

- The cat is too frightened to eat when the others are in the feeding area.

🐾 The cat is too fearful to use the litter tray and may soil the house.

🐾 The cat is no longer willing to approach you, because of fear of being attacked by the other animals in the house.

🐾 You come back into the house to see signs of conflict: tufts of fur, or blood.

🐾 The aggressor is patrolling an area of the house so that the victim only has a small area of living space.

If any one of these signs is evident, you must get help from a pet behaviour counsellor. If there is more than one sign, or if expert help fails, then you have no choice but to consider re-homing the victim cat.

Remember to put your cat's happiness before your own.

*Ah! Cats are a mysterious kind of folk. There is
more passing in their minds than we are aware of.*
Sir Walter Scott
(1771–1832)

6

how to solve
your cat problems

One popular author has it that men are from Mars and women from Venus. If this were literally true, then cats would be from Mercury – the smaller, hotter planet!

Considering how different our two species are, the relationship between humans and cats works extraordinarily well most of the time. Humans provide food and shelter and cats graciously accept them. All they are required to do is to repay their humans with affection and the beauty of their presence.

Nowadays, a cat is often a human's best friend. They fit into modern life rather better than dogs. Cats don't bark or make noise. They don't need daily exercise and they are usually clean in their toilet habits.

Solving modern problems

Yet even the modern cat sometimes has quite a stressful life. While cats can and do live in colonies, they are not pack animals. Individual cats vary in their ability to deal with group living. In the household of compulsive cat rescuers, there are usually three or four unhappy animals living under the bed, creeping out only when no other cats are around to take a hurried meal.

This is the extreme, of course, but even households with four or five cats may put intolerable stress upon a cat that is not happy with group living.

The solitary indoor cat, whose owner is out all day, is stressed by the opposite situation: hours of boredom with nothing to do and no contact with any living being. Food comes daily in the bowl, and there is no opportunity for the cat to express its predatory instinct. Such cats may turn playfully on their humans, using them as prey!

When your relationship with your cat does run into trouble, it usually occurs within one of four main areas: toilet arrangements, scratching, eating or aggression. The first difficulty is the most severe one, because the odour of cat urine is powerful, pungent and very difficult to erase.

Why cats mark with scent

Sometimes cats start going outside the litter tray – not because they are unhappy with litter arrangements, but because they have started marking their territory. You can tell the difference by the location of the marks.

A cat going outside its litter tray because it is unhappy about the toilet arrangements will usually go either near the tray (or near its old position) or in a secluded place, such as behind furniture. A cat that is territory marking will urinate in a more obvious position, and the urine mark will usually be on a vertical rather than a horizontal object. If you see them doing it, they are usually spraying urine from a standing, not a squatting, position.

If your cat feels that its core territory is no longer safe, it will respond by setting up stronger territory marks within the house. To reduce its own anxiety, it will start leaving 'Tabby's here' notices in order to deter other cats, dogs, wildlife or human intruders. These notices are usually urine marks made by spraying, but they may also be faeces left uncovered.

The scent of these marks makes the cat feel less anxious. It provides the same feeling of reassurance for the cat as we humans feel when we close the curtains, keeping in the light and shutting out the night world outside. Your cat is putting down a small marker that keeps out what is frightening and keeps in what is comforting – for a cat.

Interpreting the signs

Sadly, we humans rarely recognize these 'Tabby's here' messages for what they are. We often react with anger and alarm, rather than love and comfort. Some owners interpret them as insults; others get so upset that they punish the cat. Naturally, the cat becomes even more frightened. Its home feels positively dangerous when it is shared with a punishing human. The cat responds in the only way it knows: by putting up even more and stronger reassurance messages.

We can learn to interpret some of these messages by taking a careful look at where such messages occur.

If the cat is leaving spray marks or faeces under or near the window, the likelihood is that something in the garden outside is frightening it. Maybe, through the window, it can see a fox or a local cat bully. Marks at the inside of a door may have been left because your cat can smell dogs or other cats that have passed by or even urine-marked on the other side.

Another common reason for marking is when an intruding cat uses the cat flap – often a hungry stray coming in to steal your cat's dinner. Quite naturally, your cat is upset by this intrusion into its own core territory. It may spray near the cat flap, or if it is horribly upset, it may go upstairs and do it on your bed.

Humans often think this spraying is an insult, yet it is just the reverse. The cat, anxious and insecure, is going to the place that smells of its loved one. It mixes its scent with your odour – and feels happier as a result. Cats that go on the bed are telling you that they love you and need your help.

Other intruders that upset cats include builders, friends or people you have invited to a party. Even cat-sitters or neighbours coming in to feed the cat while you are away can be upsetting.

Normally your cat may be friendly to the woman next door. It may greet her happily when she is in her garden. But if she comes into the house when you are away, even to leave regular food, a sensitive cat may feel she is intruding into its private space.

Other upsetting occurrences for sensitive cats include new furniture, a new baby, or even a change in routine (for instance, if their owner suddenly starts working night shifts instead of the accustomed day shifts).

Coping with scent marking

Your first move must be to clean up the territory marks. Wash or dry-clean any marked materials. Never use disinfectants or any scented household liquids on floors or carpets. Instead, scrub well with biological washing powder or liquid, or with products sold by a vet. Then rinse the area with plain water; this is important.

Finally, allow the area to dry or dry it with a hair-drier, and then scrub over again with surgical spirit. This is also important. Unless the area is thoroughly cleaned, your cat will simply re-mark it!

Next, either use Feliway on the marking sites or the scent from your cat's cheek and chin as described in Chapter Five. Cats do not rub where they have sprayed, and conversely, they do not spray where they have rubbed. So if the mark site smells of chin or Feliway, they will not urine-spray it.

Use the Feliway spray lavishly twice daily for at least a month. If you are stingy with it, it may not work. Also install a Feliway Diffuser in the relevant room. This may seem an expensive procedure, but almost any expense is worthwhile it it reduces spraying. Then place cat beds and cat feeding bowls at the spray sites. As we have seen, cats don't like to spray where they dine or sleep.

Finally, you have to find out what has stressed the cat, and correct the situation – see pages 120–1. If you're not sure what is causing the behaviour, get expert help from a pet behaviour counsellor.

WHY CATS SCRATCH-MARK

The other less difficult, though no less irritating, territory mark is the scratch. Scratching is natural for all cats and takes place even if the cat feels perfectly at ease.

In the house, give the cat at least one large, steady scratching post (the best are covered with sisal, not carpet), and try to discourage scratching in the rest of the home. A scratching post should be installed anywhere the cat scratches.

Double-sided sticky tape is the best way to stop furniture scratching. The cat stops scratching because it hates getting its paws sticky, and, after a week or two, the tape can be removed – though new tape may be needed when the cat realizes the furniture is free from tape! Taping your furniture may look bad, but not as bad as having it hang in shreds.

Horizontal surfaces such as carpets can be covered with see-through plastic from a DIY shop, with cooking foil, or with garden netting. A scratching post should be installed nearby as a substitute place to scratch.

Some cats scratch outside doors in order to let their owners know they want to be let in. The only way to stop this behaviour is never to let the cat in when it has scratched. It should only be let in when it has not scratched.

Shouting at a scratching cat is not a good idea. Cats often scratch in front of other cats, possibly as a competitive way of saying 'Look at me: I can scratch higher than you.' Your cat may also scratch in front of you, glancing sideways to see if this gets your attention. Shouting 'Stop that!' is attention, and bad attention is better than none.

If you think your cat is scratching as an attention-seeking device, walk immediately out of the room. Do not use a water pistol. A cat squirted in its home territory may begin to feel unsafe and start spraying – and nothing is worse than a spraying cat.

WHY CATS GET EATING DISORDERS

Most cats regulate their food intake better than humans do, but the feline world does include over-eaters, often encouraged by doting owners. Over-eating cats take less exercise and have more interest in food than ordinary cats. If your cat gets too fat, put it on a diet available from your vet, limit its intake, and do not waver. Most fat cats have a human enabler.

However, there are cats which have a serious eating disorder. These are the cats that eat strange substances like cardboard or wool, cats that chew and rip but don't swallow, and cats that just lick these odd materials. If your cat starts doing this, or even starts eating its litter, take it to the vet, because a bizarre appetite may be a sign of physical illness.

Correcting weird behaviour

If your cat is in good health, however, eating strange things such as wool or cotton is more likely to be a disorder of the natural feline hunting instinct. Siamese or related breeds are particularly prone to this behaviour, as are indoor cats with no chance to hunt prey.

Remember the hunting sequence of eye, stalk, pounce, bite, tear off skin or feathers and eat? These are cats that have become compulsive about one part of the predatory sequence: tearing off skin or feathers. Some just tear and pluck and do not swallow. Others tear and pluck and then eat.

Since ordinary cat food provides no opportunity for tearing and ripping, the cat looks for something else to satisfy this urge. It will tear, rip, chew (and sometimes eat) wool, cotton, paper, cardboard, wicker baskets and even electric cables. Cats that simply rip, tear, chew and then spit out do little harm to themselves, but those that swallow these inappropriate substances risk an internal blockage, requiring an operation.

The treatment for this behaviour is to give your cat the chance to tear and shred by feeding either dead whole, feathered turkey chicks; day-old chicks; dead whole rats; or dead furry mice (not the baby pinkies) sold frozen in pet shops for reptiles. If all else fails, buy hens with their feathers still on from a local farm shop. Wash your hands before and after feeding, because there is a slight risk of contracting salmonella.

These should be the cat's main diet, eaten in a room (like a bathroom) where blood won't get on the carpet! Although the whole idea is disgusting to humans, this may be the only way to cure your cat of a dangerous disorder If you want to add a little dry food on top of this (only a minority portion of the diet), try to do so in a foraging toy (or a small yoghurt container punched with holes), so the cat has to work to get the food out.

Because this weird behaviour is part of the hunting sequence gone wrong, it may also help to give your cat the chance to hunt, either by allowing it out of doors or by giving it a lot of predatory games where it can stalk and pounce on toys.

Reinforcing weird behaviour

Owners whose cats merely tear and chew rather than swallow weird substances often find the disorder amusing. The danger is that, if your cat is merely tearing and chewing, it may be encouraged to go further and start swallowing. Be careful to withdraw attention from a cat that is tearing and chewing. This takes nerve if your cat is chewing electric cables. But shouting 'No!', rushing over to it or picking it up will only encourage it, since all these moves provide human attention. Instead, leave the room.

While trying to cure non-eating chewing, cover wires with plastic tubes from a DIY shop. Try painting cables with Tabasco sauce or use bitter-apple spray as a deterrent. If these don't work, offer cat chews or, if necessary, some dead chicks in the diet.

Why cats bite

Under normal circumstances, cats rarely attack humans. If they dislike a person, they are far more likely to make themselves scarce. If a previously calm cat suddenly turns aggressive, it is essential to take it to the vet. A sick cat or a cat in pain may bite when handled. Pregnant cats or cats with litters are also sometimes aggressive in defence of their litters.

A kitten brought up in the wild will never become completely domesticated. These unsocialized strays might learn to live in the house, but they may continue to bite from fear when handled.

Understanding petting and biting

This is the most common occasion when otherwise friendly cats bite. Petting is very enjoyable to humans, but it is less enjoyable to cats. It relaxes us, but it can stress some cats. If your cat bites when being petted, it means it is in conflict: it wants attention but fears it, too. Your cat may want contact and love, but after a time it gets frightened. At this point, it bites or scratches suddenly.

This may be the result of a dysfunctional kittenhood, and probably this kind of cat's desire for space should be respected. Some stray cats, however, have had kittenhoods in a home but then have suffered at the hands of man while they lived in the street. After months in a safe, new home, these cats may accept petting more easily in time. But never try to hurry them.

Some cats have sensitive areas – tummy and hind parts – which produce aggression. Avoid these! Long-haired cats may have been roughly groomed in the past and may be more likely to bite or scratch if they feel threatened. On page 90, I provide instructions on how to get them used to being groomed again.

If you want to try to change this petting-and-biting behaviour, use special treats as a reward for calmness. Show your cat the treat first, then give it a little bit of petting – just calm stroking nowhere near its tummy. Your cat will be focusing on the food.

Give the treat after only a very short period of petting. If your cat swipes a claw at you, then it doesn't get the treat that it has already been shown. In this way, calmness during petting is rewarded. Slowly increase the petting time, always making sure your cat sees the treat on offer before you start.

In general, only pet your cat when it can get away: *i.e.* with no enclosed arms and probably not on a lap. Do not pick it up. Try stroking only the head and down the back. Always let the cat remove itself when it has had enough. If you can afford regular supplies, you could also make your hand smell friendly by using Felifriend spray from the vet.

Develop your relationship in other ways than petting. Non-cuddly cats will still enjoy play. Have regular play sessions with string, fishing rods and so on. The other way to develop a relationship is to use food treats to train a cat to do simple tricks of a kind that it enjoys. Greedy cats really enjoy these and will actually solicit training sessions.

Some other reasons may make your cat bite human beings.

Predatory aggression

If cats don't have enough to do (and indoor cats usually don't), attacking humans is a substitute for hunting mice. Pouncing and attacking is instinctive behaviour for cats and they really enjoy it. Give your cat more to do by following the instructions listed in Chapter Four.

If your cat already goes outside but simply enjoys pouncing on you, use sound as a discourager. Ring a small bell each time you start vacuuming (most cats loathe the vacuum cleaner), then use the bell when you see the cat about to pounce. The aim is to deter your cat from pouncing without causing it to become frightened of you.

If your cat attacks neighbours, just give them a water pistol and ask them to use it. In this case, it doesn't matter if your cat starts avoiding them.

Frustration aggression

Hand-reared kittens are sometimes unable to tolerate frustration because they were not weaned properly (see page 64). These cats have no emotional control because they were not put through this process. They have no inbuilt coping strategy for frustration, so simply lash out. They control their owners by aggression, as the owner naturally backs away.

You can turn this relationship around by clicker-training or reward-training the cat. If necessary, attach a soft object to a stick in order to move the cat gently off a chair (and avoid getting hurt).

Aggressive play

Sometimes people encourage kittens to do rough games but dislike it when the cat has grown up and wields a stronger claw or more painful bite. But by then the cat has rough games in its repertoire. The rule is that games stop immediately if your cat hurts you.

Attention-seeking biting

Some cats nip their owner's legs when they want something. The answer is to withdraw attention. Don't shout, don't wince and don't cry. Just walk out of the room immediately and stay out for three or four minutes.

Transferred aggression

Occasionally, a usually docile cat will attack its owner because it is aroused by something else. If it's watching another cat through a window, it cannot help itself; its aggression has to be expressed, even on the person nearby, who may well be its owner.

STRESS PAWPOINTS

* *Other outside cats, dogs or wildlife.* Stop leaving food down indoors or close the cat flap. Wash down the outside of doors daily to clean up any smells left by neighbouring cats, etc.

* *Sight of animals.* Block off the sight of the potential threat by covering the window. Prevent strange cats from sitting on window boxes or window-sills by covering boxes and sills with netting.

* *Indoor cats.* This can mean that your cats are fighting, or just that one feels pressured. For a good diagnosis and solutions, contact a behaviour counsellor. Consider re-homing.

* *New objects.* Treat new objects with Feliway or mark them with the cat's own scent from cheek or chin.

- *Builders and decorators*. Put the cat in a cattery during building works. Use Feliway in the newly decorated room or in the new house.

- *Visitors*. Cats will sometimes spray after visitors. Consider putting your cat in a cattery at holiday times or during visits.

- *Spraying for attention*. Get expert help!

- *New cat flap*. Get rid of it or shut it down.

- *Electrical items*. When they heat up, they may emit odours. Try Feliway if you can use it safely!

- *Another cat's health*. Medical problems in the cat's companion cat may produce spraying. Check any companion cat's health with your vet.

*Nothing is more playful than a young cat,
nor more grave than an old one.*

THOMAS FULLER
(1608–1661)

🐾

7

how to pamper
your elderly cat

Like humans, cats live longer nowadays. And like humans, their personalities remain the same. Your cat is still a cat, even if, in its old age, it is less likely to spend hours outside in cold weather hunting mice in the hedgerows. But if it enjoyed hunting in its prime, it will still enjoy it even if its prey is more likely to be butterflies than rabbits.

If your cat entirely loses its predatory instinct and no longer takes an interest in watching birds and mice, it may be suffering, or at least may not be very well. Old age should not alter its individual personality much, either. An aloof cat may become slightly less aloof but it is unlikely to turn into a cuddly teddy bear of a feline.

Giving your cat a long life

If they avoid the dangerous infections of cat flu, FIV (feline immunodeficiency virus), feline leukaemia and other fatal diseases, and do not get run over by cars, cats can often reach the age of fifteen. A few, with super-survivor genes, get past the age of twenty and may even pass the age of thirty.

If you want your cat to survive into old age, then vaccination is essential if it is allowed out of the house. It is now possible to vaccinate against feline leukaemia as well as cat flu and feline panleucopaenia, a kind of viral gastro-enteritis.

There is also a vaccine against chlamydia that is useful if your cat lives in an area full of disease-ridden strays. If you are a cat rescuer likely to have stray cats passing through your house on the way to a rescue shelter, your own cats should be protected by chlamydia vaccinations.

For a better idea of how fast cats age, see page 153.

How to protect against disease

Prompt treatment of disease is essential for emotional and mental well-being in old age – both for humans and for cats. If your cat shows signs of emotional illness (geriatric confusion), this may be a side-effect of illness rather than a permanent condition.

In the past, both cats and dogs were often put down because their owners could not, or did not want to, pay out large sums for veterinary treatment. Pet insurance has benefited many cats and dogs, making veterinary treatment affordable, even for people on a relatively small income.

Be sure to choose an insurer that will continue to insure your cat after a certain age. No insurer will take on an already elderly cat, and some of the cheaper insurers will actually refuse to insure animals after the age of eight years old. Sadly, in this, as in so many other aspects of life, you get what you pay for.

Health care for cats has improved immeasurably in the last decade, and it is now possible to measure cat blood pressure and detect many diseases at an early stage. Most good veterinary clinics now offer both regular vaccinations and regular health checks for elderly cats.

Blood tests can detect the early stages of kidney disease, liver and thyroid disease. This preventive treatment is not covered by insurance, but any subsequent veterinary treatment that are needed as a result of these tests should be.

Do not hesitate to seek a second opinion for all serious or chronic health problems. Just as general-practitioner doctors refer patients to specialist consultants, so ordinary vets can refer their animal patients to specialist vets. This is a much more effective way of getting additional help for a cat with a specific health problem than simply changing vets. The veterinary department of the local university or a nearby specialist veterinary hospital will be able to offer more up-to-date diagnosis and treatment.

The only contra-indication for veterinary treatment is when old age is allied to serious disease. Each round of treatment is stressful for a cat that cannot understand why this is happening. Do not strive indefinitely to keep a sick cat alive. Quality of life should always be seriously considered before starting long, invasive and difficult (for the cat) treatment.

Preventing illness

Regular worming against tapeworm is important for cats that catch mice. Control of fleas is also important, since tapeworms are spread via fleas. Most people don't realize that treating the animal is not enough.

It is essential to spray the house at regular intervals, otherwise a reservoir of flea eggs and larvae grow up into fleas, which bite the cat. Flea allergy, in which cats groom themselves bald and sore, is a serious disorder, yet many owners still don't treat the house, confining themselves to treating the pet. There are now very effective anti-flea preparations for house and cat, many with growth inhibitors that attack the flea's ability to reproduce.

Dental care is the other area where many owners fall short. Middle-aged cats often develop dental problems. Their teeth get coated with calculus, which inflames the gums. Each time your cat is vaccinated, your vet should check the condition of its teeth. If your cat seems keen to eat but draws back when it starts eating, the cause might be tooth pain.

In theory, it is possible to learn how to brush your cat's teeth. But failing regular brushing, consider dental food or dental chews or even cleaning under an anaesthetic. Cats with a history of cat flu sometimes develop chronic gingivitis. Use of steroids or even complete extraction of all teeth may be the treatments of last resort.

How to nurture your old cat

Special diets are now available for elderly cats or cats with health or digestive troubles. Some of these are prescription diets, available only from vets, designed for cats with a chronic problem such as kidney disease or cystitis, allergy or food intolerance, or bowel or digestive difficulties. Alas, pet insurance will rarely cover the cost of a continuing special diet, but the diet will help your cat stay healthier and live longer.

There are also prescription slimming diets for cats that need to lose weight. In general, most cats seem able to balance their diet so that they eat what they need without getting fat. Yet a small proportion of cats are fatties – whether because of their genes or the over-indulgence of their owners.

Detecting problems in fatties

Fat cats are much more likely to suffer from diabetes. In addition, too much weight is apt to worsen many diseases such as arthritis and breathing difficulties.

Just like fat humans, fat cats become less energetic, so they do less and put on even more weight. Food may become so important to their lives that they start living to eat. Doting owners contribute to their obesity by sharing human meals with their fat, furry friend.

This is called enabling. We owners with fat cats enable them to stay that way by letting, even encouraging, them to eat too much. The only kind action is to put the cat on a diet, always under veterinary supervision, and limit its food intake rigorously.

Never starve a fat cat. If a fat cat suddenly stops eating, its liver function may fail. Weight should always be lost gradually. Prescription diet foods, usually bulked out by extra fibre weighed in a daily portion, are the best way of slimming down a fatty. A new slimming diet may need to be introduced gradually and mixed with the previous food to ensure that it's being eaten. If your cat regularly supplements its diet by entering other houses and raiding other cats' food, or even turning over the local dustbins, it may need to be an indoor cat while it diets.

Understanding your elderly cat's needs

Whatever its size, the older cat has probably become more vocal, as it has learned that human beings respond to sound rather than body language. If it begins to wail, becomes restless and loses weight while eating well, it should be checked for thyroid disease by a vet.

Sometimes very old cats cry in the night, probably out of geriatric anxiety and a desire for a cuddle. But a change in vocal tone should always be investigated.

Elderly cats will also sleep more. One conscientious feline researcher did a day's study watch on an elderly cat, staying awake and noting all its movements for a full twenty-four hours. While she struggled to stay awake, the cat slept in peaceful serenity for sixteen of those hours.

Some elderly cats (by no means the majority) suffer from arthritis. Never give your cat a human painkiller, since cats react differently to drugs than humans. However, a vet can prescribe appropriate drugs to reduce pain.

Provide ramps up to high places, and site beds and food bowls carefully. A food bowl raised on a telephone directory will help cats with an arthritic neck. A heated pad or even a heated tunnel provides comfort for stiff and ageing limbs. If you can't get your cat its own heated bed, prepare to share not just the outside, but also the inside, of your own.

Elderly cats will also need help with grooming. They may no longer be able to reach difficult areas, such as along the back. Regular clipping of claws may be necessary; ask your vet's nurse to show you how.

Minimizing stress

Many old cats adapt surprisingly well. The idea that an elderly cat will not be able to handle a change of house, a major change of routine or a new person in the household is unfounded. Elderly cats in good health seem to be able to handle the change perfectly well and to thrive in the new environment. There is no real reason, therefore, why older cats should be put down when their owners die. Given the chance, they can enjoy a new home.

Change they can handle, but not big, new stresses. With its playfulness and desire for games, a new kitten may discompose an older cat unused to companions. Your cat's early history will be important here. If it was brought up in a crowded cat household and has been used to other cats in its present home, even in old age it will probably be able to adapt to a newcomer.

Stress for the elderly can be diminished by the lavish use of Feliway and the sensible use of a cattery when the household is being disrupted by building works. Using the same cattery for each visit and supplying your own Feliway spray should make the cat's stay more tolerable.

Old cats show an increased ability to manage humans! Many cat owners find themselves becoming devoted and obedient servants to their elderly feline – moving over in the bed to offer more room under the duvet, holding the cat's tail or stroking it while it eats, giving up the warmest seat by the radiator, and generally responding to elderly vocal demands for instant attention! There is no need to be embarrassed by this. Your cat probably feels that this is its right as a member (in its eyes) of a superior species.

And, on reflection, perhaps it really isn't altogether bad that we humans, so arrogantly sure of our place at the top of an evolutionary tree, should pause and consider our own status. A relationship with a cat involves a little bit of human humility as well as a lot of human love.

QUALITY OF LIFE PAWPOINTS

❧ Is your cat still enjoying its food?

❧ Does your cat still play if you invite it?

❧ Is it able to control its bowel or bladder?

❧ Can it get to litter tray, food and bed?

❧ Can it still wash the easy-to-reach areas of its body?

❧ Is it suffering from frequent fits, vomiting, or other disorders?

❧ Is it in pain?

❧ Does it often need veterinary interventions or procedures such as injections?

❧ What does your vet recommend?

HOW FELINE YEARS COMPARE WITH HUMAN YEARS

	CAT YEARS	HUMAN YEARS
Middle-aged	9	52
Old but active	11	60
	14	72
Old	16	80
Very old	20	96

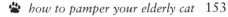

A WORD ABOUT DISABLED CATS

In the past, disabled cats were almost always put down. Today, we know that disabled cats, like disabled people, can lead happy lives. In most ways they function just like healthy cats. They simply need a bit more help.

Most disabled cats should be kept indoors, or with access only to a high-fenced garden. They are more vulnerable to traffic, dogs and predators, even in home territory.

Deaf cats respond well to hand signs; choose your own, but be consistent. They may also respond to vibrations. Try clapping with palms slightly cupped; this makes a vibration which the cat may 'hear' through its body. To recall a cat from the garden in the dark, use a torch to flash the signal.

Blind cats cope better than blind humans because they have superior hearing and scenting abilities. Whiskers also become feelers for new territory.

A study of blind cats concluded that they have no difficulty making their needs known. If disorientated, they often sit and howl to be picked up. They still know where the fridge is! Blind cats play with noisy toys.

Make life easier for your blind cat by keeping furniture and the litter tray in the same places. Cats are incredibly good at mapping out areas, and learn their own home area rapidly. Leave doors either shut or fully open. Use fireguards near all open fires.

Wobbly cats with poor coordination, sight problems, spasms or deformed front legs can also lead enjoyable lives. Litter trays must be 'untippable', since puss may need to lean against a side while using it. Even cats with urinary incontinence (as a result of a car accident) can be helped. It's possible to learn how to express the urine, which will stop the incontinence. Get your vet to demonstrate.

USEFUL NUMBERS & ACKNOWLEDGEMENTS

For good information sheets about feline diseases, cat boarding, cat rescue, and some feline behaviour problems: send an sae to the Feline Advisory Bureau, Taeselbury, High St, Tisbury, Wilts SP3 6LD. Tel: 01747 871872. Website www.fabcats.org

The Association of Pet Behaviour Counsellors, PO Box 46, Worcester WR8 9YS. Tel: 01386 751151. Vet's referral required. A counsellor will visit your home to assess the problem.

For cat and dog behaviour courses and books: The Centre of Applied Pet Ethology, PO Box 6, Fortrose, Ross-shire IV10 8WB. Tel: 157 0800 783 0817. For courses: www.coape.co.uk. For books: www.pet.f9.co.uk

For a kitten socialization pack: contact Headstart for Kittens, The Blue Cross, Shilton

Rd, Burford OX18 4PF. Tel: 01993 825500. Order online from www.bluecross. org.uk

Bereavement helpline: the SCAS Blue Cross line on tel: 0800 096 660 will help you come to terms with losing your pet.

My own website, www.celiahaddon.co.uk offers help with cat problems and includes a special section on disabled pets. I regret that I cannot promise to reply to all inquiries.

I would like to thank the Universities Federation for Animal Welfare (The Old School, Brewhouse Hill, Wheathampstead, Hertfordshire AL4 8AN, UK) for permission to use plates 4, 5, 7, 8, 16, and 22 from *An Ethogram for Behavioural Studies of the Domestic Cat (Felis Silvestris catus L.)* by the UK Cat Behaviour Working Group, UFAW, 1995.

INDEX

A

age comparisons,
    feline-human, 153
aggression,
    against humans, 39, 130-5
    body language, 36-8
    fighting, 28, 43, 105
arthritis, 147, 149
attention-seeking, 39, 40, 45,
    52, 101, 125, 135
    discouragement, 70-1

B

bad behaviour, elimination of:
    see counselling *and* training
beds, 107, 123, 149
bereavement helpline, 155
biting, 130-5
blindness, 156-7
body language, 36-41, 48
boredom, 117
    alleviation of, 85-7
breathing difficulties, 79, 80-1,
    89, 147
brushing, 83, 90-1

C

calls: *see* vocalizations
car travel, 66
cat flaps, 120, 137
catnip, 85
changes in routine, 121, 150
chewing,
    discouragement of, 129

claw-clipping, 67, 149
claw messages, 41
cleaning scent marks, 122-3
counselling, 123, 136, 154

D

danger, avoidance of, 28-9, 68
deafness, 89, 156
dental care, 67, 145
disabled cats, 155, 156-7
disorders, inherited, 77-9, 88
dogs, 58-9, 102-3
'domestication', 12-13, 18, 19

E

ear messages, 36-7
eating,
    disorders, 126-9
    scavenging, 19
    see also food *and* special diets
elderly cats, 46-7, 50, 139-53
eye contact, 37-8

F

faeces, 28, 119, 120
    see also middening
faults, pedigree 88
fear, 112-13
    body language, 37-8
    of brushing, 83, 90-1
    of petting/stroking, 130-3
    and territorial marking,
        118-23
Feliway, 49, 66, 105-6, 122-3,
    136, 137, 150, 151
Felifriend, 132
feral cats/strays, 18, 21, 57, 120

fleas, control of, 144
food, 86-7;
    see also special diets
food bowls, 107, 123, 149
food treats, 67, 73
fright: see fear
frustration, 64, 134
furniture damage:
    see scratching

G
gardens as territory, 97-9
grooming,
    by cats, 43, 52, 83, 112, 149
    by humans, 67
    see also brushing

H
hairballs, 83, 89
hearing, 46
hiding, 112
houses,
    acclimatization to, 59
    moving house, 29, 150
    as territory, 96-7
hunting,
    instinctiveness, 22-3,
    62-3, 80
    predatory sequence, 23-5, 30
    results of prevention, 126-9
    see also play-hunting

I
inbreeding, pedigree, 77-9
incontinence, 157
indoor cats: see pedigree cats
information/contacts, 154-5

instincts, 20-30
insurance, 142, 146

K
kittens, 57-61, 154-5
    training, 62-73

L
latrine areas, outdoor, 27
leashes, 67
life expectancy, 140-1
litter trays, 63, 107-11, 113
long-haired cats, 82-3, 89, 131

M
middening, 44, 53

N
neighbours, 121, 134
neutering, 21, 22

O
obesity, 146-8
old cats: see elderly cats
other cats, relations with, 104-8
    companion cats, 137
    kittens/elderly cats, 150

P
paw messages, 41
pedigree cats, 60-1, 66,
    76-89
petting/stroking, 48-9, 102,
    130-3
play, 72
    rough play, 67-8, 70, 135
    toys 85-6, 133

play-hunting, 23, 25-6
punishment: *see* rewards/
    non-rewards

Q
quality of life, 144, 152;
    see also boredom: alleviation

R
reassurance by humans, 38-9
    see also Feliway
re-homing, signs of need
    for, 112-13
reproduction:
    see sexual behaviour
rewards/non-rewards, 69-73
roads, 98
rolling, 39
rubbing, 40, 50, 100, 102

S
safety, need for, 26-8
scent marks/messages, 35,
    40, 42-5, 50-1, 100-2,
    104, 122-3
scratching, 44-5, 50, 71,
    99, 101
    discouragement of, 85,
    124-5
sensitive body areas, 39, 131
sexual behaviour, 20-2
shows, 76, 78
sitting places, 86
sleep, 148-9
social living, adaptation to,
    57-8, 116-17
    see also 'domestication'

solitary nature, 15, 105
spaying, 21
special diets, 146-8
spraying, 44, 51, 120-3, 125
squat marking, 51
stress, causes/relief of, 136-7, 144
stroking: *see* petting/stroking

T
tail position messages, 40-1
territories, 15-16, 27, 96-103
    marking, 28, 50, 53,
    98-101, 118-25
thyroid disease, 148
tickling, 39
tom cats, 21-2, 51
toys, 85-6, 133
training, 63, 65-72, 87
travelling boxes, 66

U
urine, 28, 117, 118
    see also spraying

V
vaccinations, 141
veterinary care, 106, 142-5
visitors, 137
vocalizations, 7, 35, 46-49,
    52-3, 70, 81

W
weaning, 64
whiskers, 35
white cats, 89
wild cats, African, 14-18
wool-sucking, 81